Art Nouveau Clip Art
for Machine Embroidery

DOVER PUBLICATIONS, INC. | Mineola, New York

Art Nouveau Clip Art for Machine Embroidery

In this book you will find a collection of rare, authentic Art Nouveau designs. These images have been carefully chosen, cleaned and prepped to give you the best quality images to use with your electronic embroidery design-making software. This unique publication helps you skip the time-consuming scanning and cleaning of images, and let's you jump right to the fun part—pattern making and sewing out!

What's in the book:

The black-and-white version shows the file that you can use in your design-making program, to create the sewable pattern.

The book is a visual index of all of the files that are on the accompanying CD. In the upper left or right hand corner of each index page are the image numbers that correspond to the equivalent files on the CD.

For every image there are different color ideas for each design.

Next to each color idea is a list of the colors that are used in the design. The number refers to the Isacord thread color number.

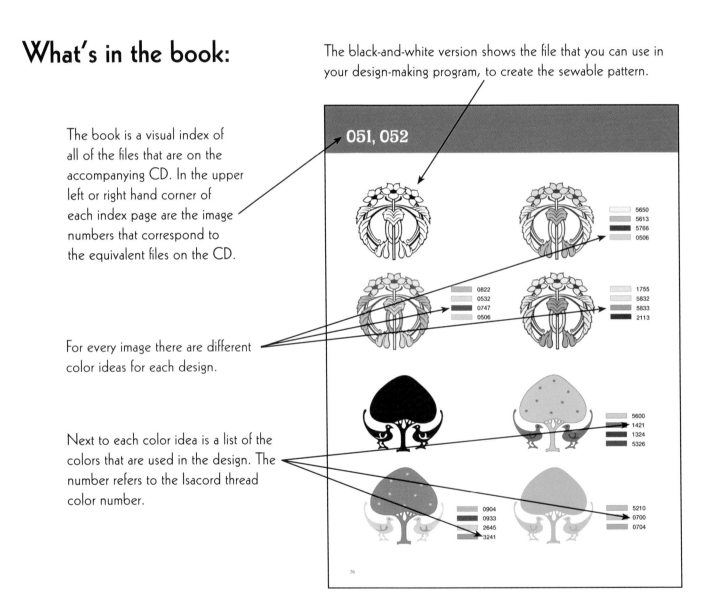

On the accompanying CD you will find a thread conversion chart, which helps you choose the appropriate thread color from four different manufacturers.

What's on the CD:

The outline versions of the images can be used with many design-making programs to create sewable patterns. Consult your program's instruction manual for specific instructions. There are both JPG and vector versions of these images on the CD.

The mass versions of the images can be used with most design-making programs to create sewable patterns. There are JPG and vector versions on the CD.

There are multiple color versions of each design on the CD. In addition to using them as a source for color ideas, these JPG images can be used as clip art for any crafts or graphics project. These files are located in the "Color JPG" folder.

Here is a finished, sewn-out pattern that was made using Brother's PE Design® software program, and Dover clip art.

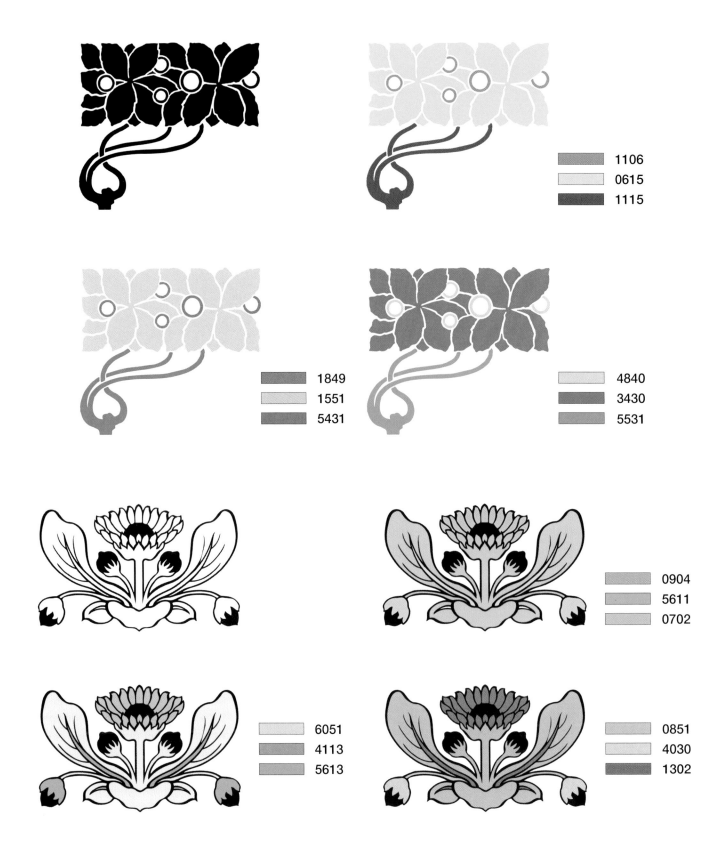

1106
0615
1115

1849
1551
5431

4840
3430
5531

0904
5611
0702

6051
4113
5613

0851
4030
1302

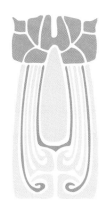

2640
0506
0842

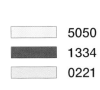

5050
1334
0221

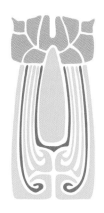

5600
5324
1430

0900
1123
0532

0506
0726
0150

0936
0232
0345

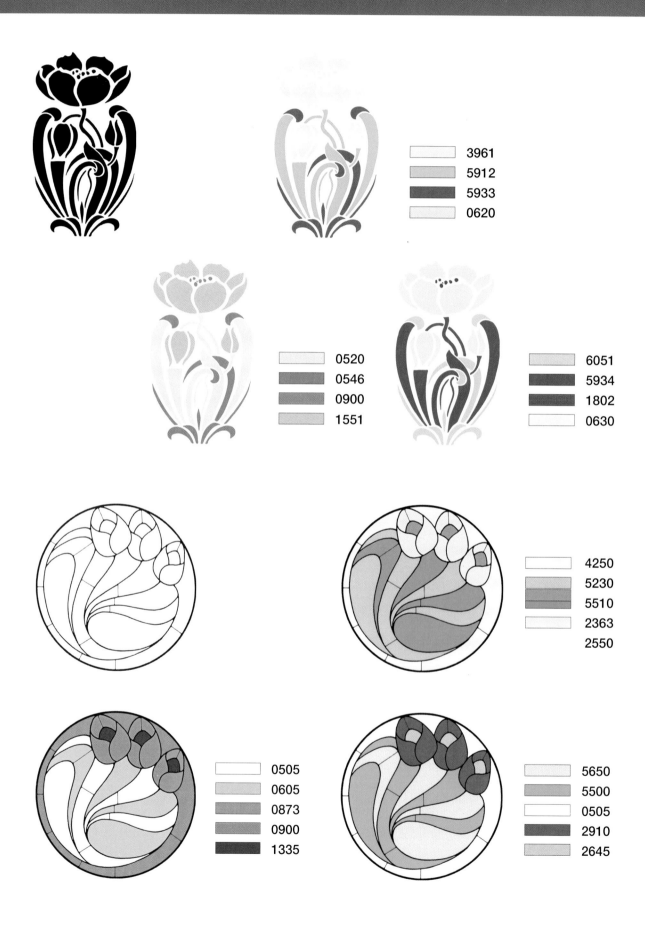

3961
5912
5933
0620

0520
0546
0900
1551

6051
5934
1802
0630

4250
5230
5510
2363
2550

0505
0605
0873
0900
1335

5650
5500
0505
2910
2645

1106	1140
1099	0842
1855	1313

3040	1120
5840	5050

3961	3040
0713	5050

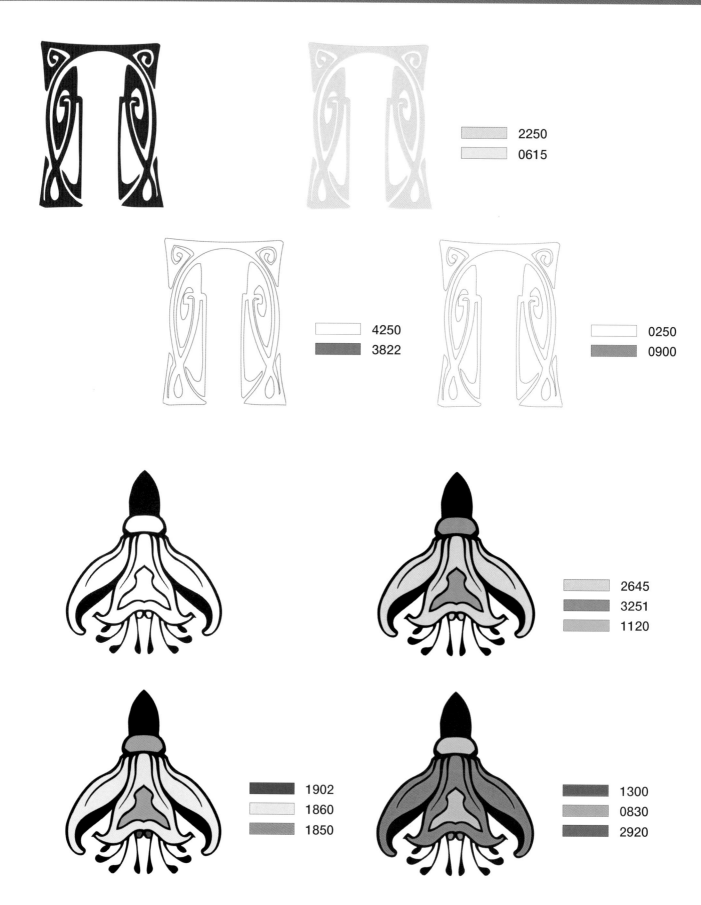

2250
0615

4250
3822

0250
0900

2645
3251
1120

1902
1860
1850

1300
0830
2920

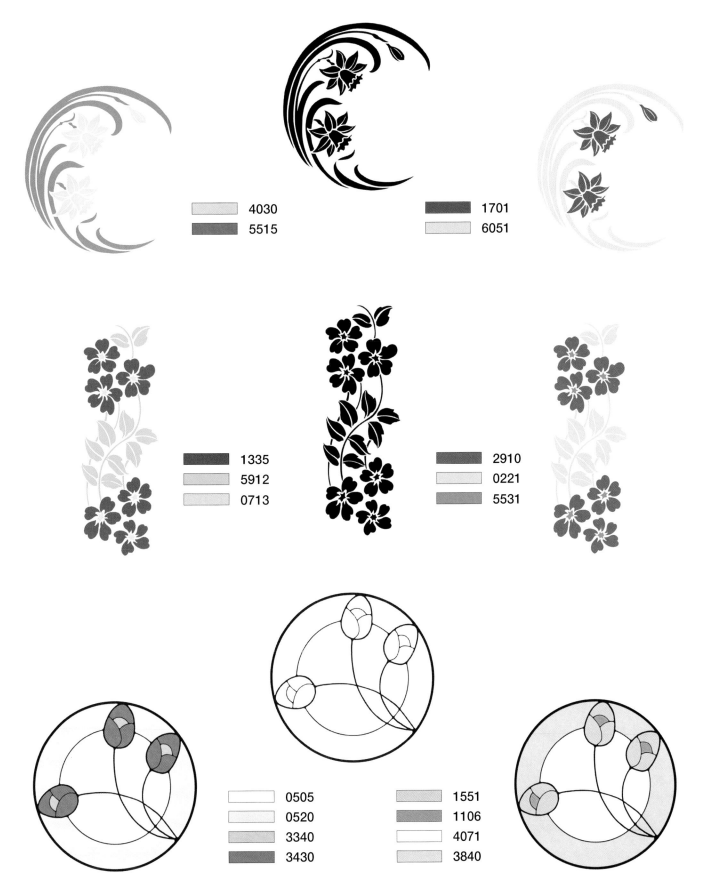

4030
5515

1701
6051

1335
5912
0713

2910
0221
5531

0505
0520
3340
3430

1551
1106
4071
3840

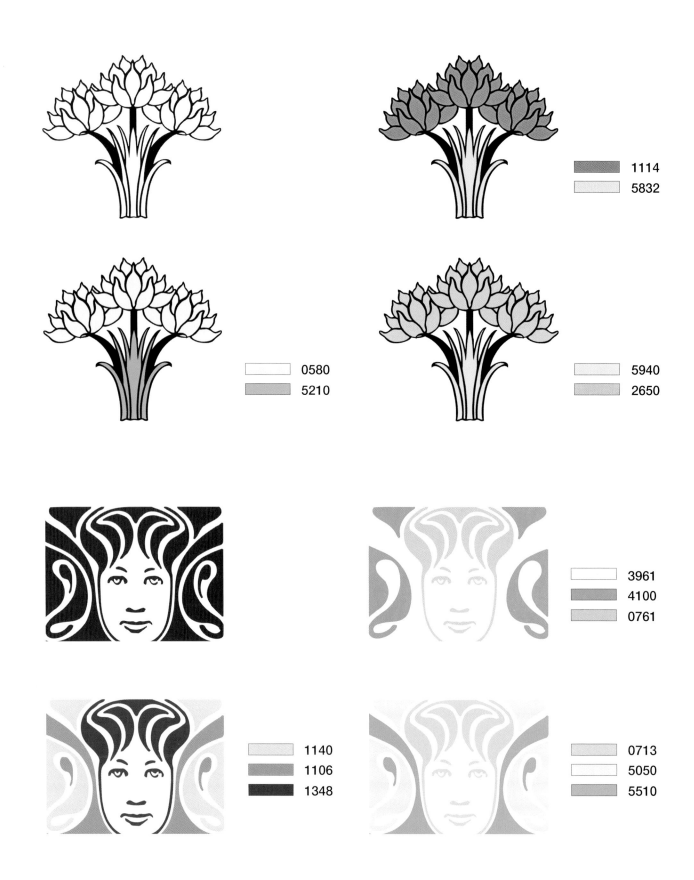

1114
5832

0580
5210

5940
2650

3961
4100
0761

1140
1106
1348

0713
5050
5510

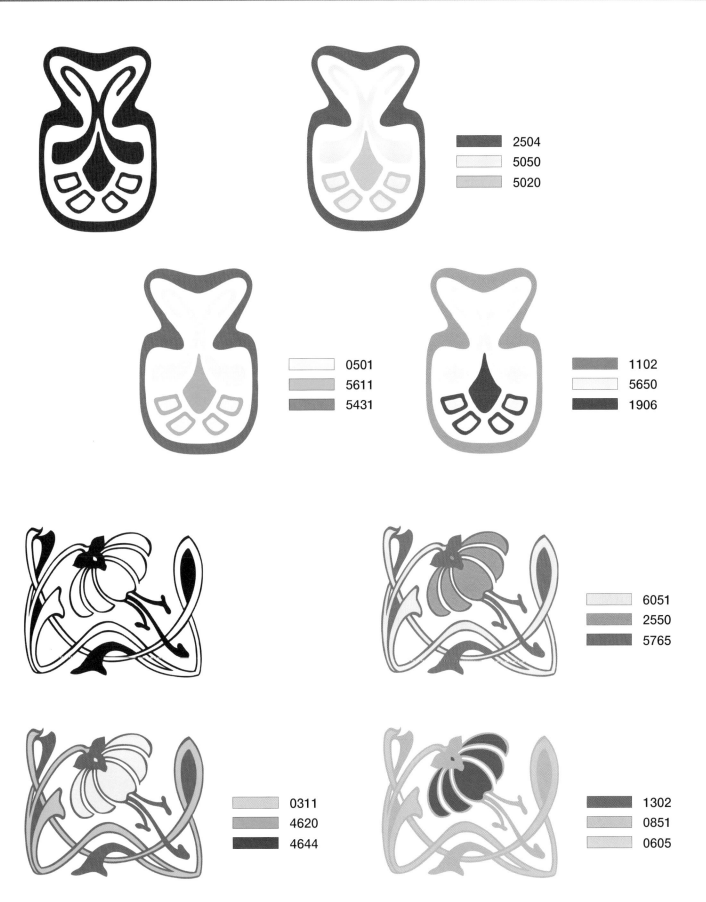

2504
5050
5020

0501
5611
5431

1102
5650
1906

6051
2550
5765

0311
4620
4644

1302
0851
0605

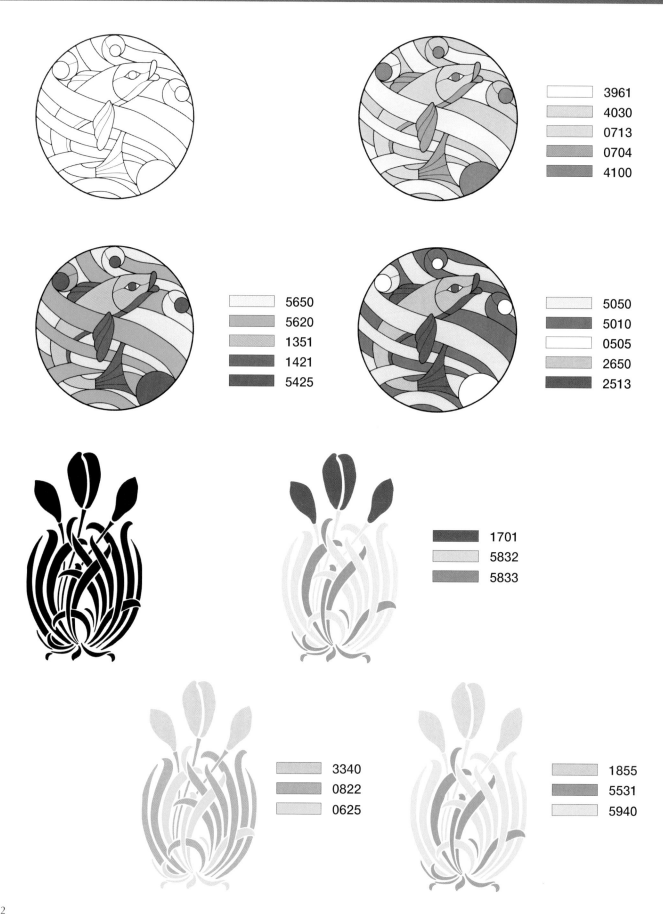

	5470		3820
	1106		1120

	5611		2640
	5650		6051
	0590		5833
	1860		0900

	0866		0761
	0870		0941
	0112		1055

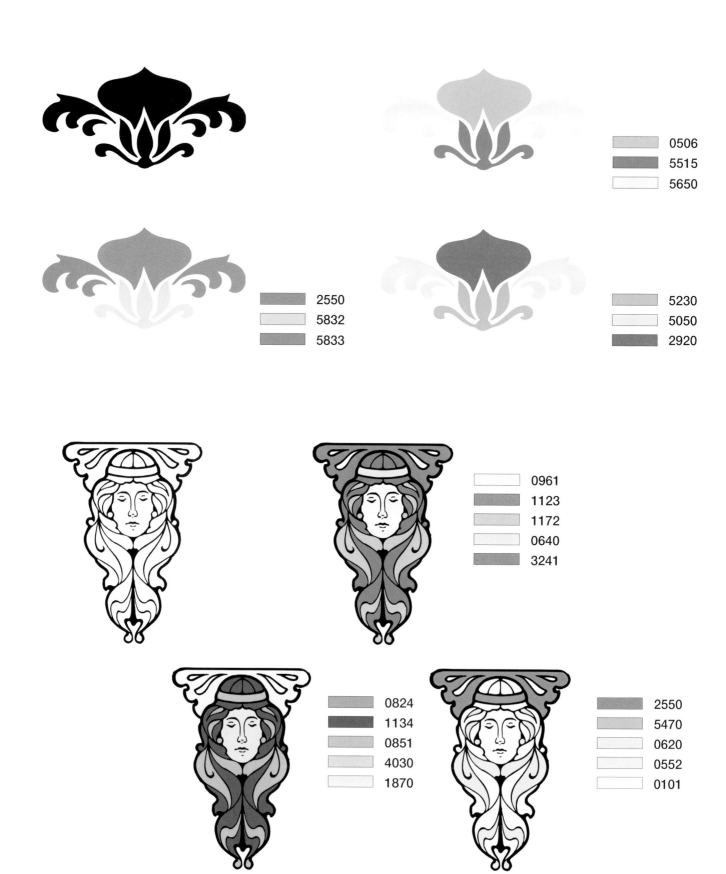

0506
5515
5650

2550
5832
5833

5230
5050
2920

0961
1123
1172
0640
3241

0824
1134
0851
4030
1870

2550
5470
0620
0552
0101

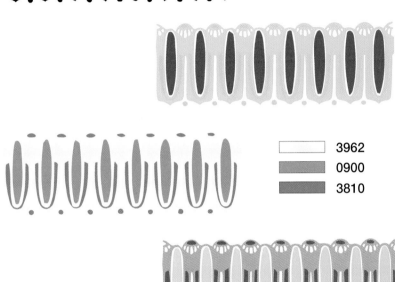

	5600
	1902
	0506

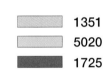

	3962
	0900
	3810

	1351
	5020
	1725

  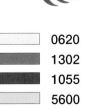  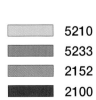 

	0620		5210		5513
	1302		5233		5940
	1055		2152		0605
	5600		2100		2600

2640	
5620	

0605	
5515	

5912		0610	
5415		1099	
0221		0933	

6051		3040	
5531		3211	
0501		5050	
1950		5210	
2166		1701	

	5500
	5513
	2241

	5411
	5940
	2611

	5912
	5415
	0221

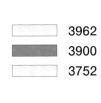

	3962
	3900
	3752

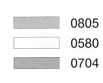

	0805
	0580
	0704

	2100
	0605
	4071

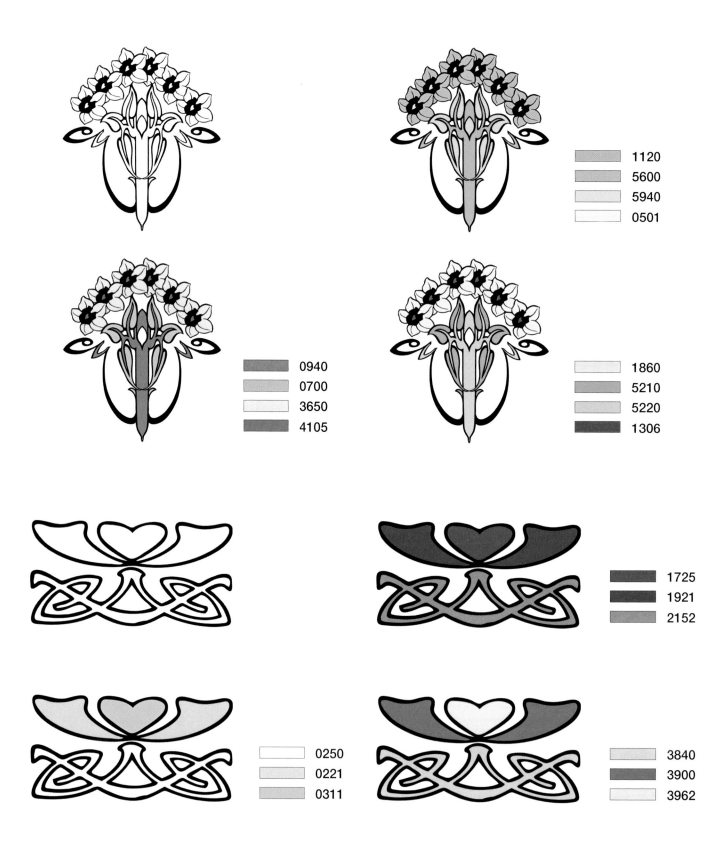

	1120
	5600
	5940
	0501

	0940
	0700
	3650
	4105

	1860
	5210
	5220
	1306

	1725
	1921
	2152

	0250
	0221
	0311

	3840
	3900
	3962

0900		5531		0936	
0932		5832		0232	
0532		0442		0345	

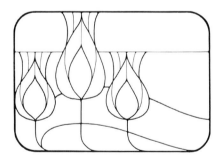

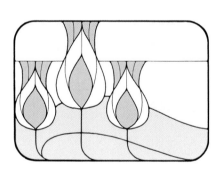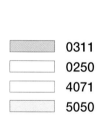

0311	
0250	
4071	
5050	

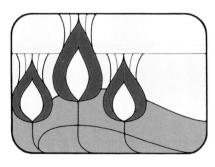

2171	
2053	
1306	
0640	

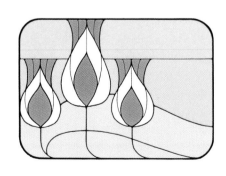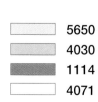

5650	
4030	
1114	
4071	

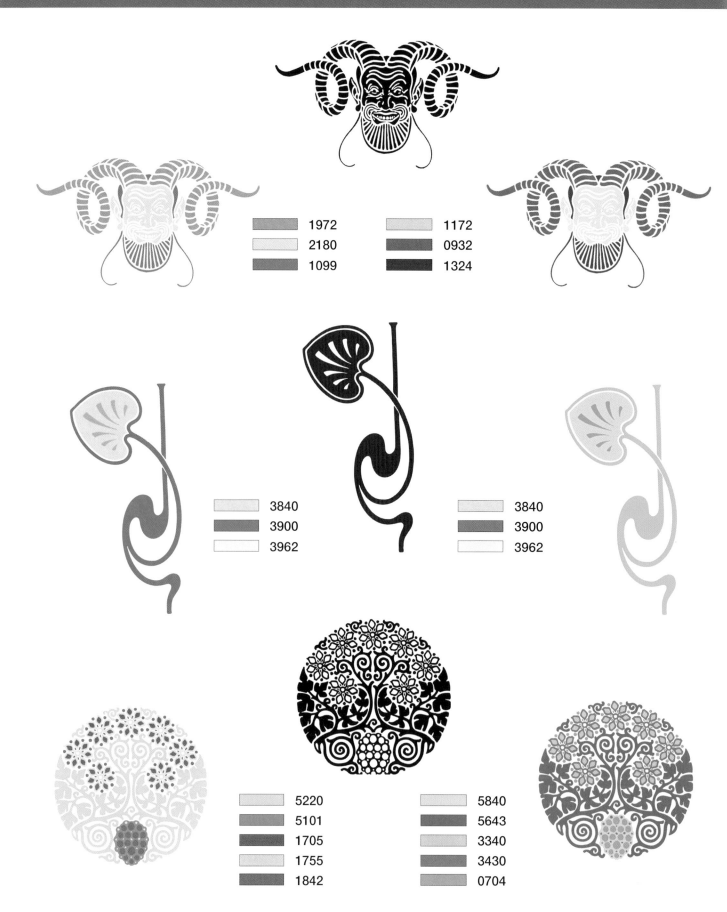

1972	1172
2180	0932
1099	1324

3840	3840
3900	3900
3962	3962

5220	5840
5101	5643
1705	3340
1755	3430
1842	0704

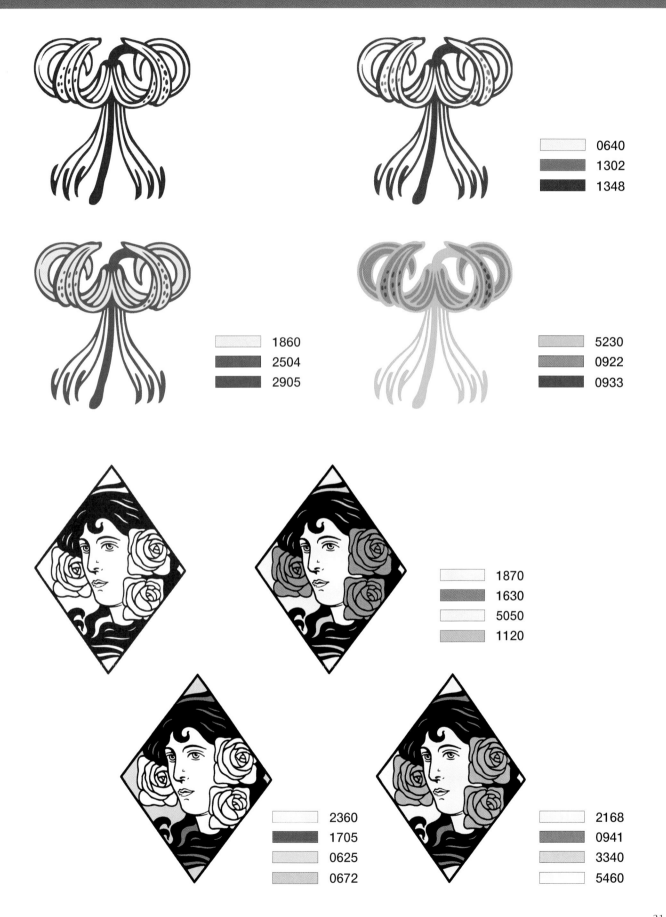

0640
1302
1348

1860
2504
2905

5230
0922
0933

1870
1630
5050
1120

2360
1705
0625
0672

2168
0941
3340
5460

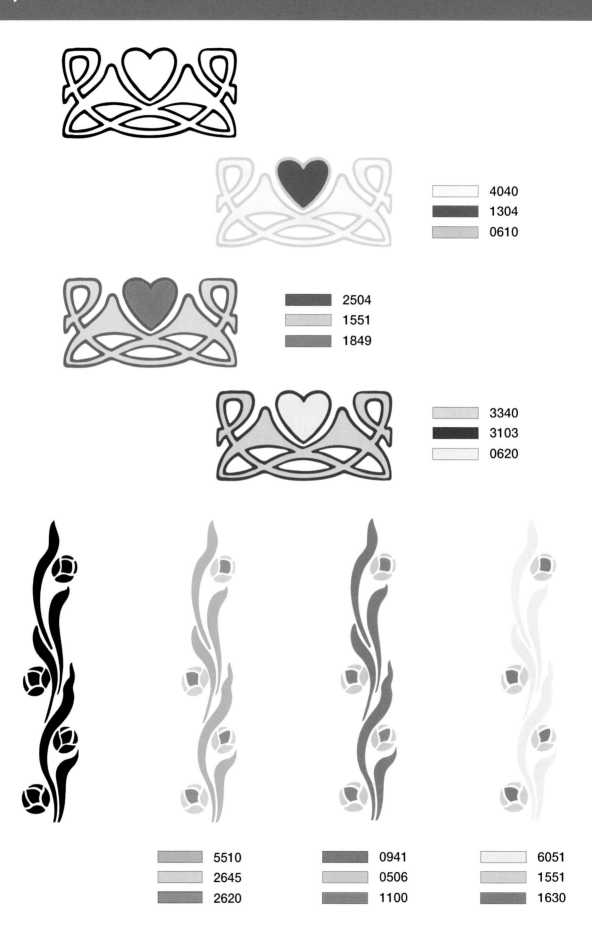

4040
1304
0610

2504
1551
1849

3340
3103
0620

5510
2645
2620

0941
0506
1100

6051
1551
1630

 3543   4250

3752 4420

3910 4400

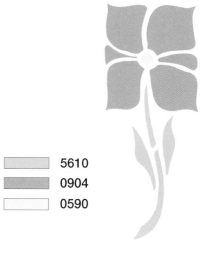

5411 5610

1906 0904

1860 0590

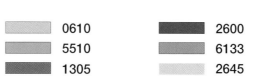

0610 2600

5510 6133

1305 2645

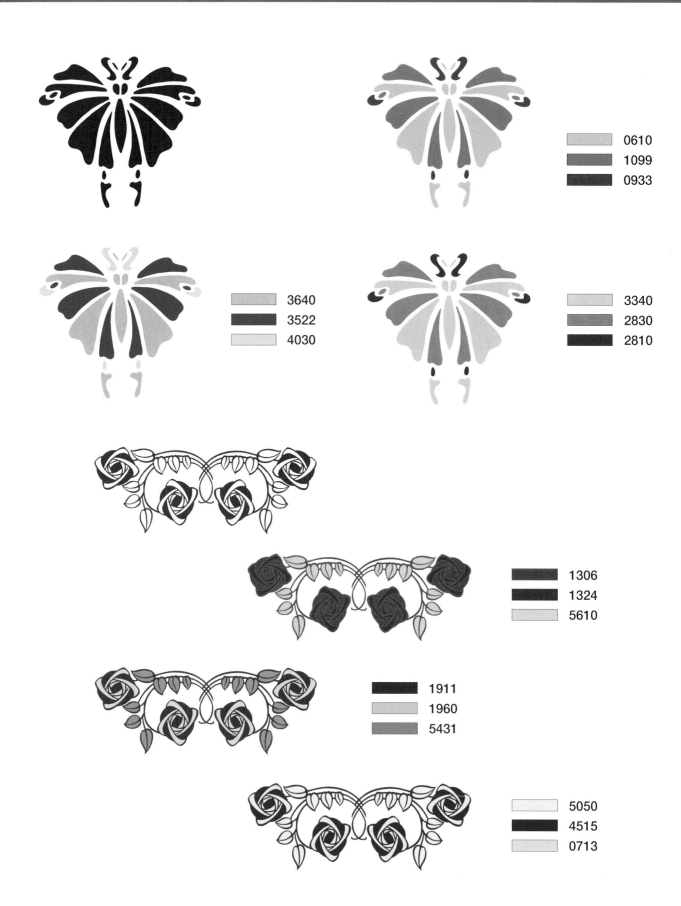

0610
1099
0933

3640
3522
4030

3340
2830
2810

1306
1324
5610

1911
1960
5431

5050
4515
0713

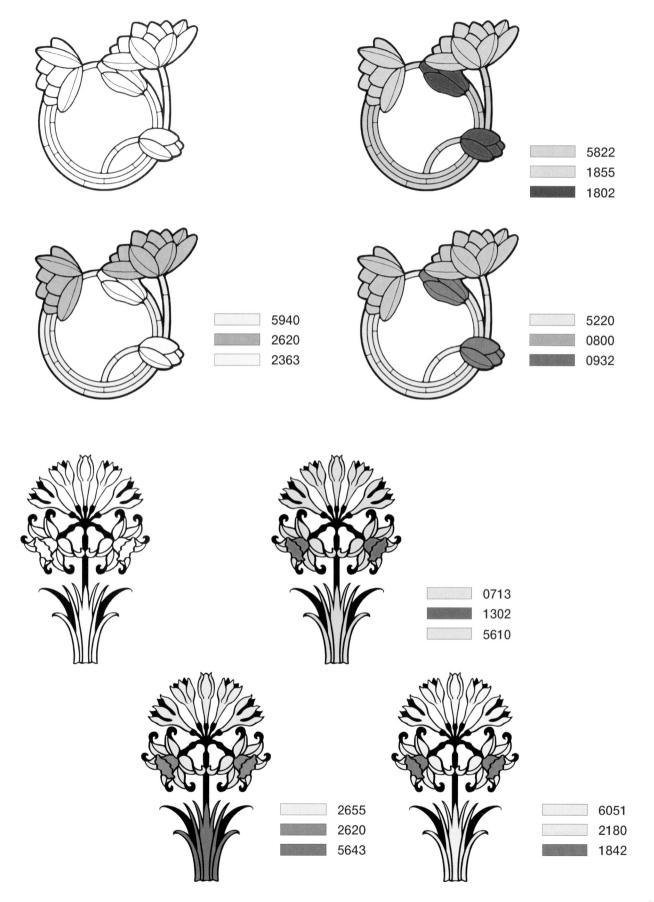

5822
1855
1802

5940
2620
2363

5220
0800
0932

0713
1302
5610

2655
2620
5643

6051
2180
1842

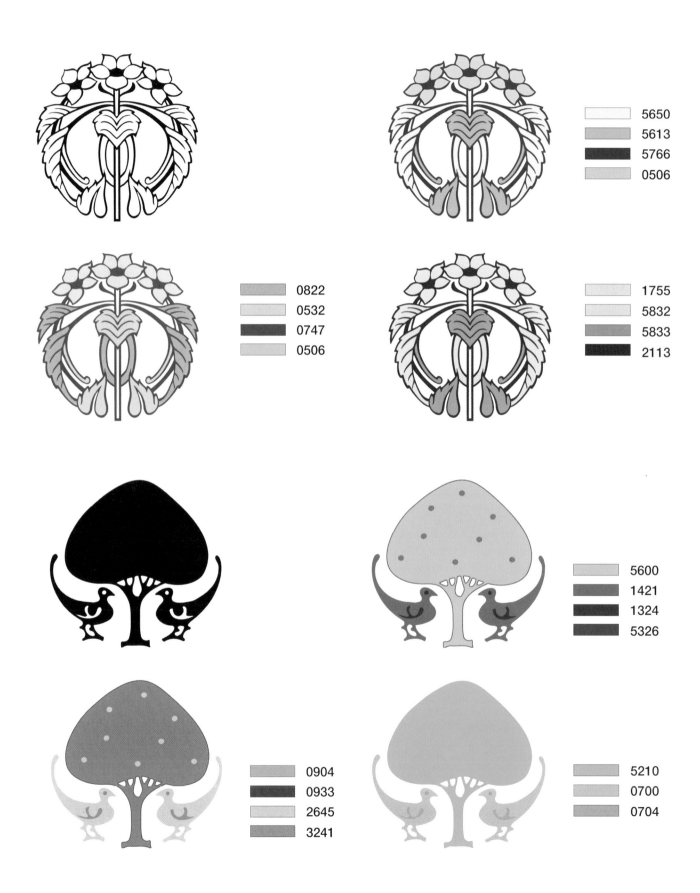

	5650
	5613
	5766
	0506

	0822
	0532
	0747
	0506

	1755
	5832
	5833
	2113

	5600
	1421
	1324
	5326

	0904
	0933
	2645
	3241

	5210
	0700
	0704

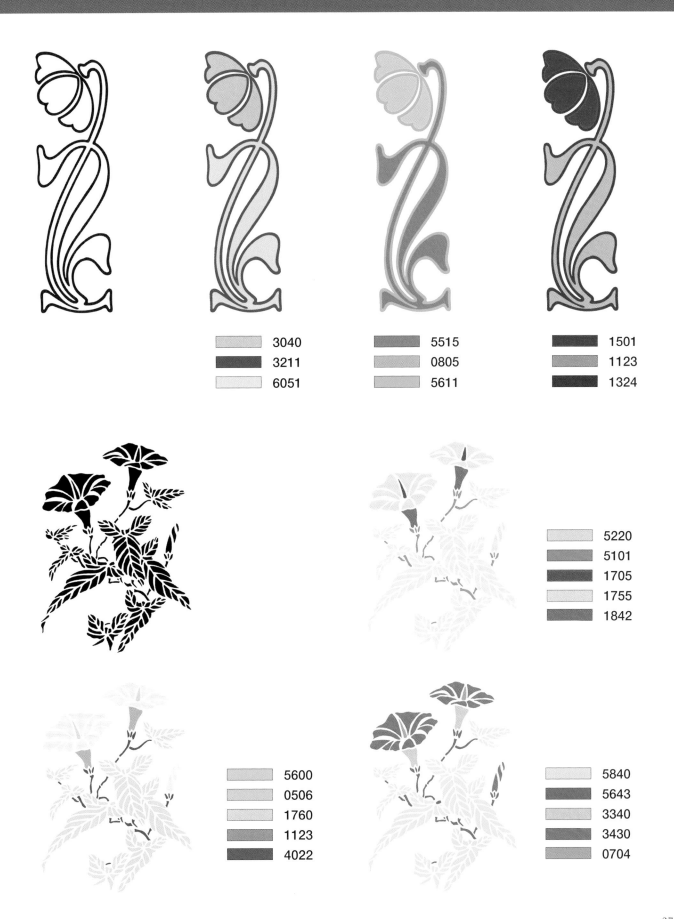

3040
3211
6051

5515
0805
5611

1501
1123
1324

5220
5101
1705
1755
1842

5600
0506
1760
1123
4022

5840
5643
3340
3430
0704

	3040		5610
	2711		1802
			1911

	5230		0713
	5050		1302
	2920		5610

	1120		5115
	1099		4643
	1324		5832

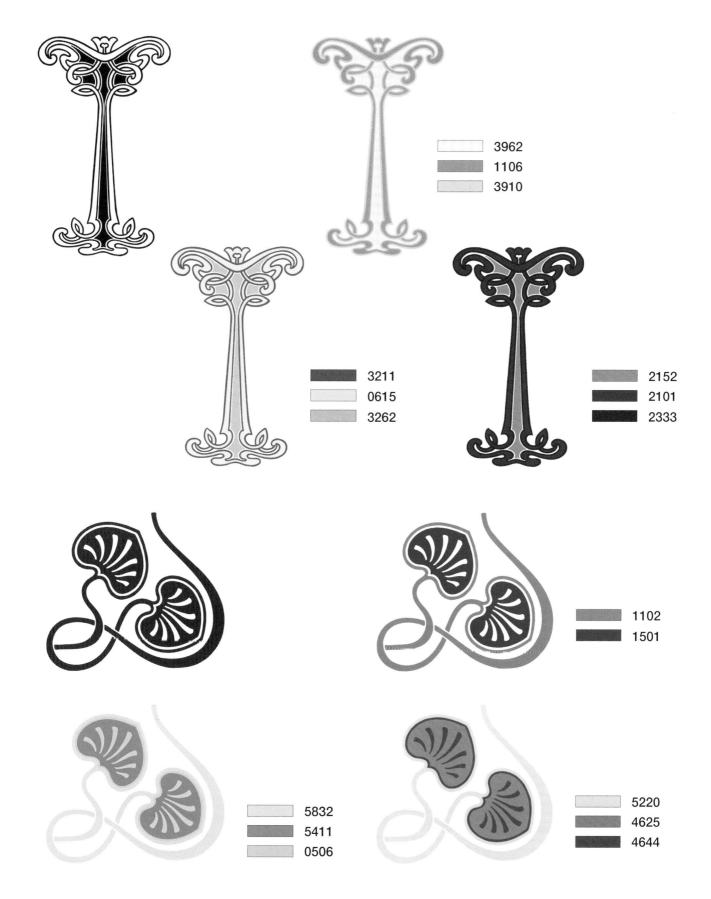

3962
1106
3910

3211
0615
3262

2152
2101
2333

1102
1501

5832
5411
0506

5220
4625
4644

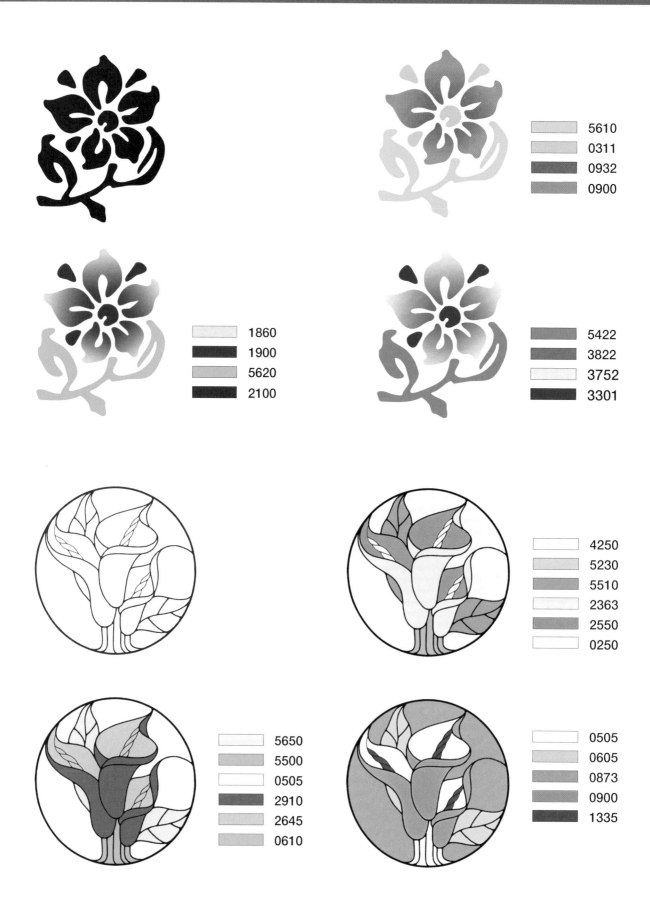

5610
0311
0932
0900

1860
1900
5620
2100

5422
3822
3752
3301

4250
5230
5510
2363
2550
0250

5650
5500
0505
2910
2645
0610

0505
0605
0873
0900
1335

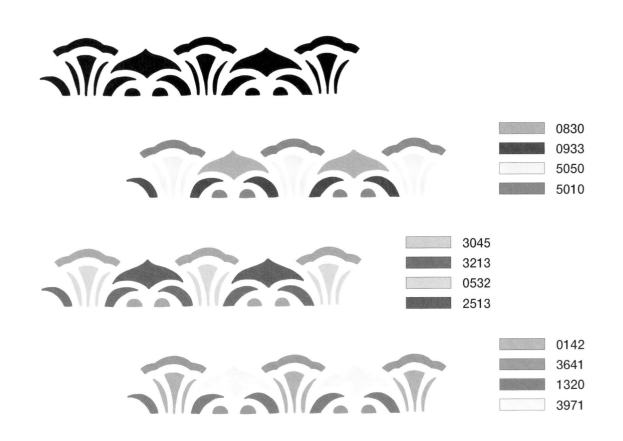

0830
0933
5050
5010

3045
3213
0532
2513

0142
3641
1320
3971

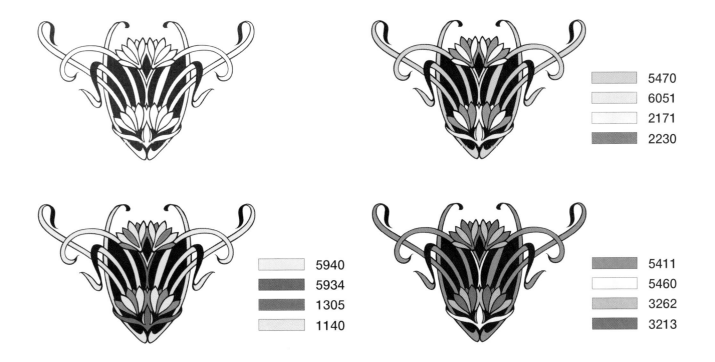

5470
6051
2171
2230

5940
5934
1305
1140

5411
5460
3262
3213

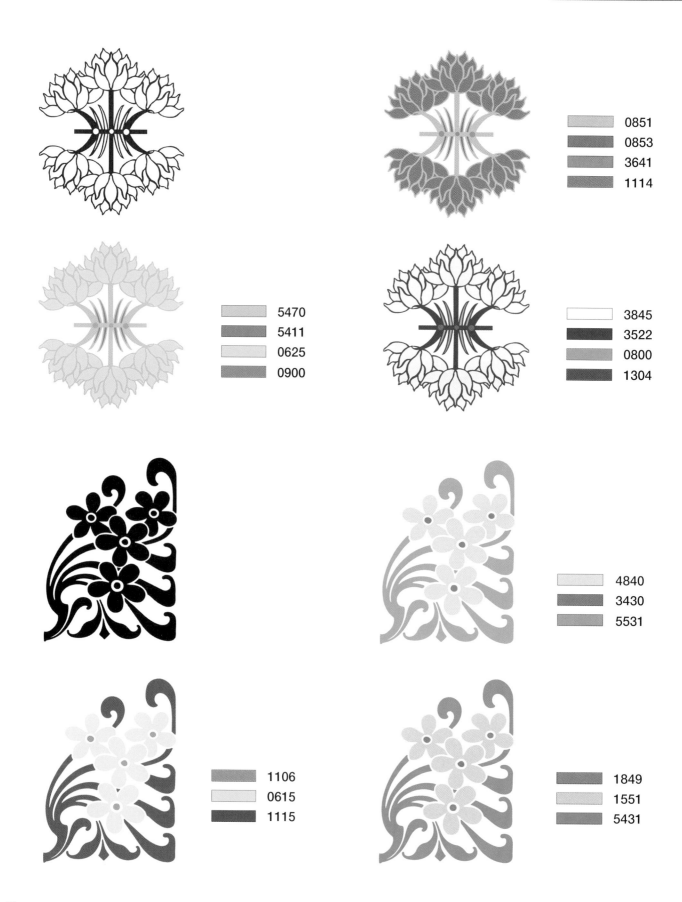

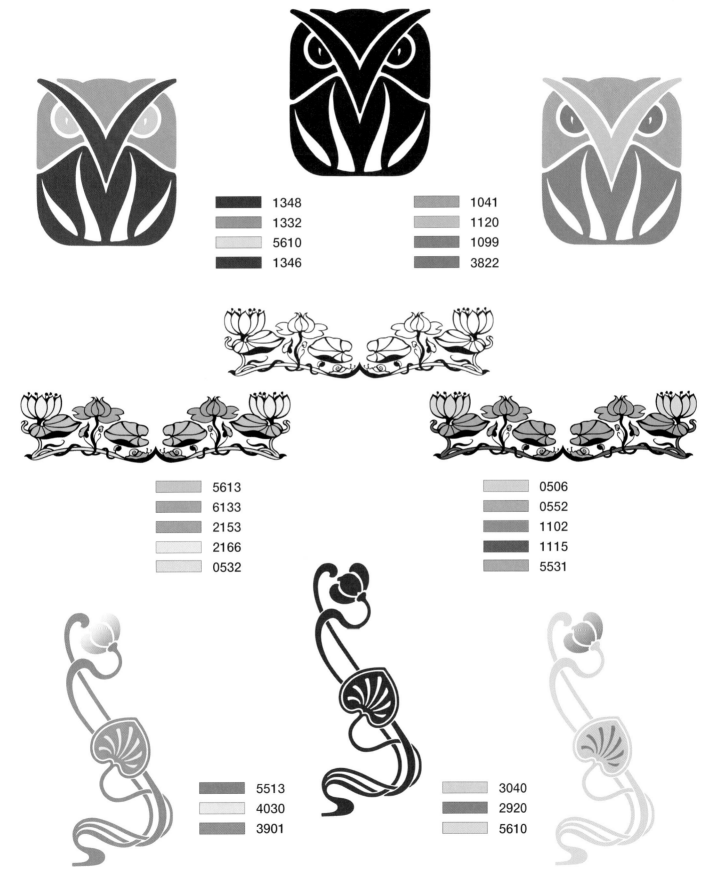

1348	1041
1332	1120
5610	1099
1346	3822

5613	0506
6133	0552
2153	1102
2166	1115
0532	5531

5513	3040
4030	2920
3901	5610

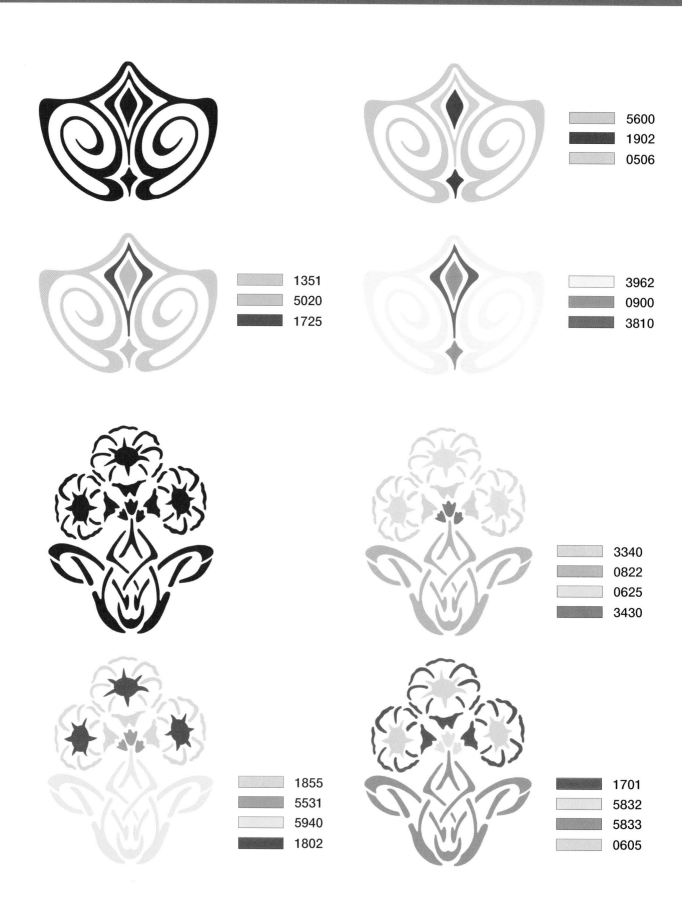

5600
1902
0506

1351
5020
1725

3962
0900
3810

3340
0822
0625
3430

1855
5531
5940
1802

1701
5832
5833
0605

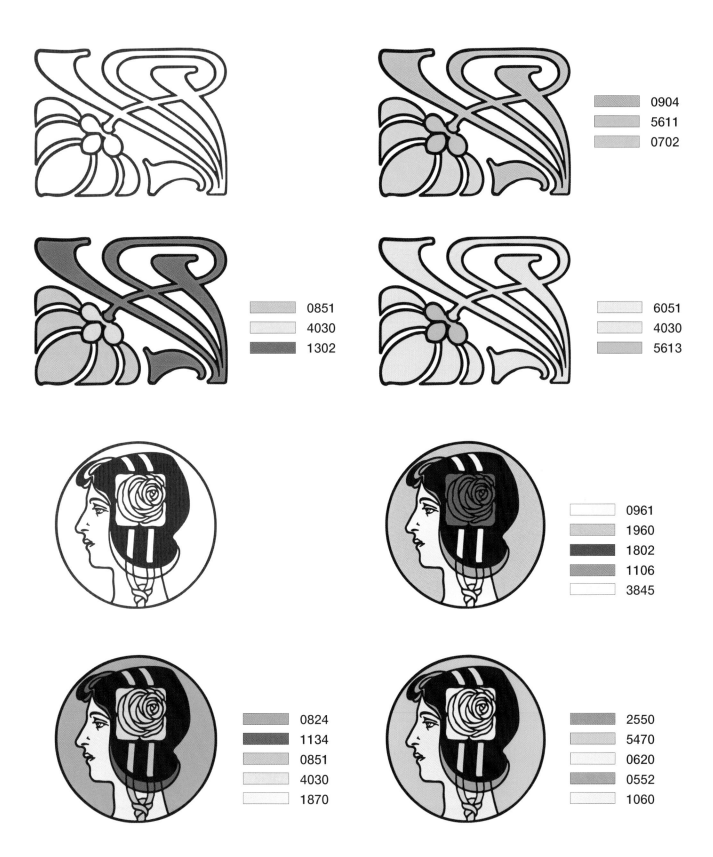

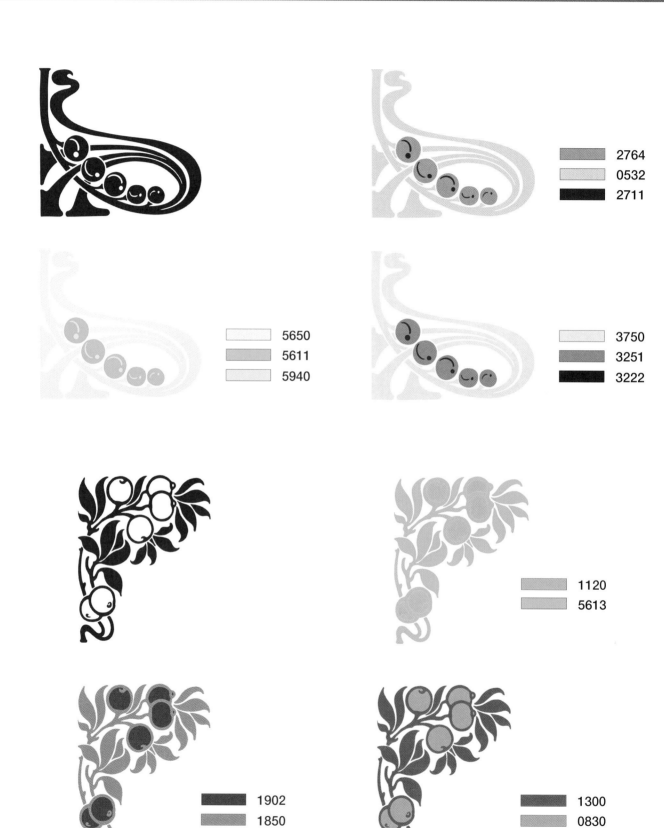

2764
0532
2711

5650
5611
5940

3750
3251
3222

1120
5613

1902
1850

1300
0830

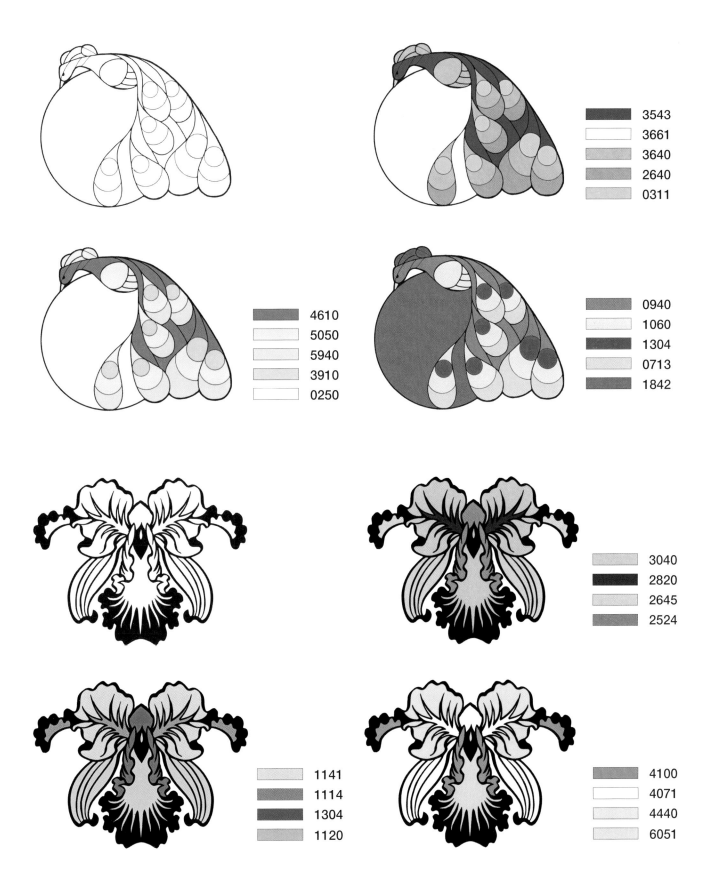

3543
3661
3640
2640
0311

4610
5050
5940
3910
0250

0940
1060
1304
0713
1842

3040
2820
2645
2524

1141
1114
1304
1120

4100
4071
4440
6051

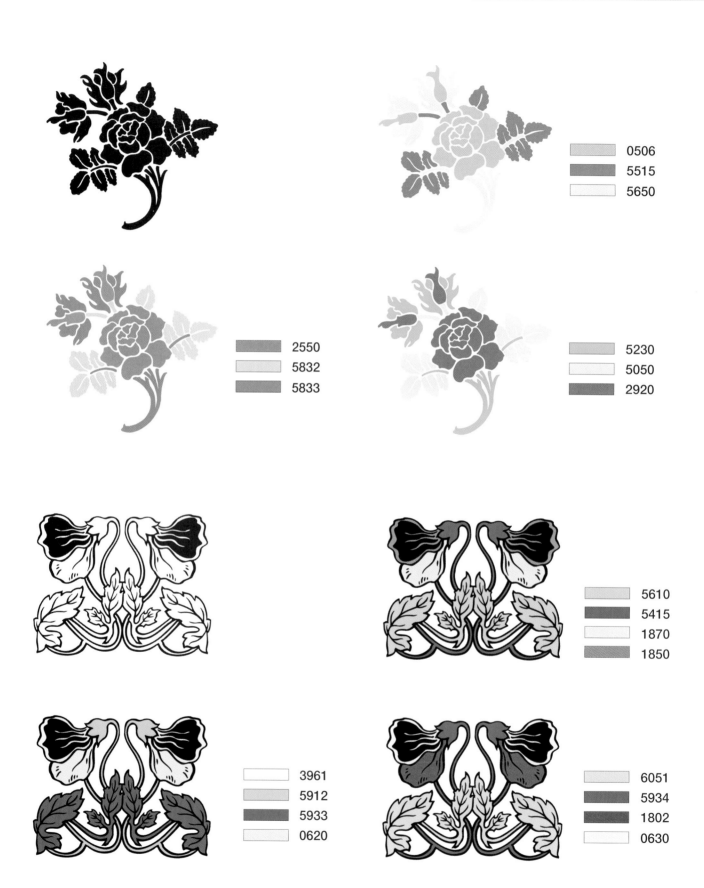

0506
5515
5650

2550
5832
5833

5230
5050
2920

5610
5415
1870
1850

3961
5912
5933
0620

6051
5934
1802
0630

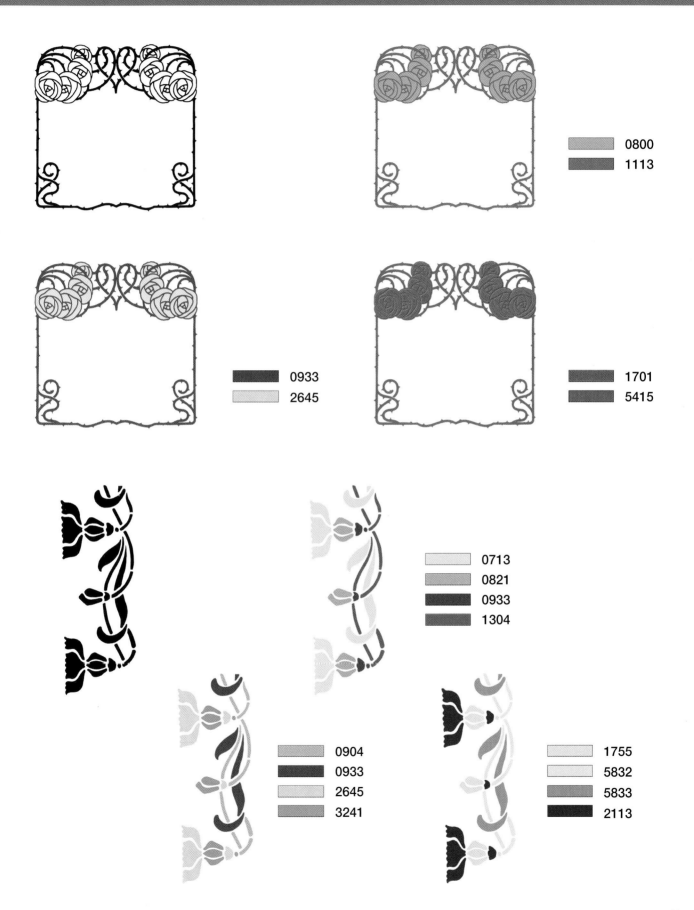

0800
1113

0933
2645

1701
5415

0713
0821
0933
1304

0904
0933
2645
3241

1755
5832
5833
2113

1120
5600
5940
0501

0940
0700
3650
4105

1860
5210
5220
1306

1102
0702
5832
5934

0822
0532
0747
0506

1755
5832
5833
2113

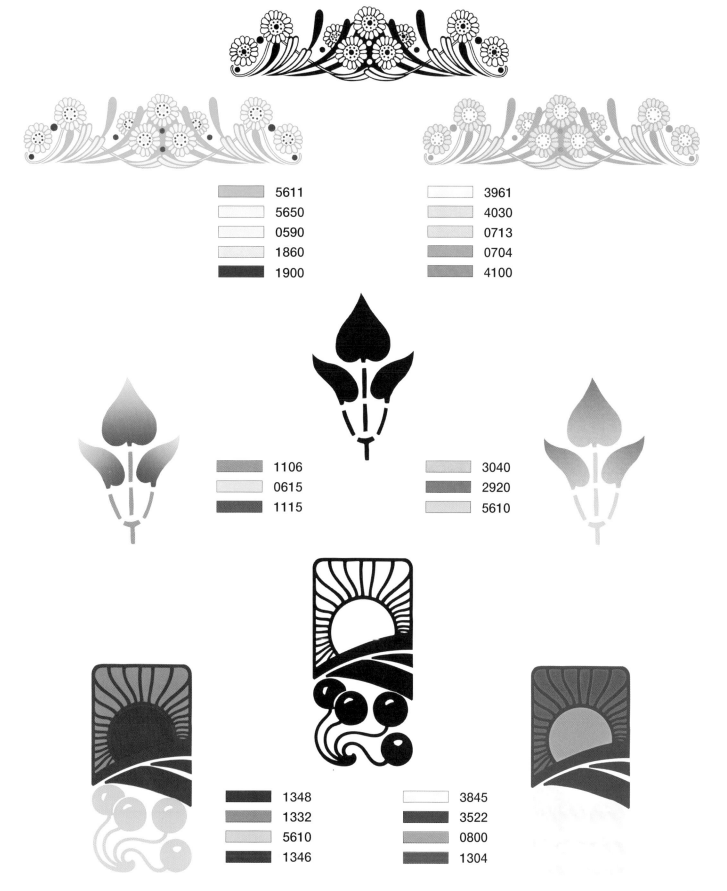

5611	3961
5650	4030
0590	0713
1860	0704
1900	4100

1106	3040
0615	2920
1115	5610

1348	3845
1332	3522
5610	0800
1346	1304

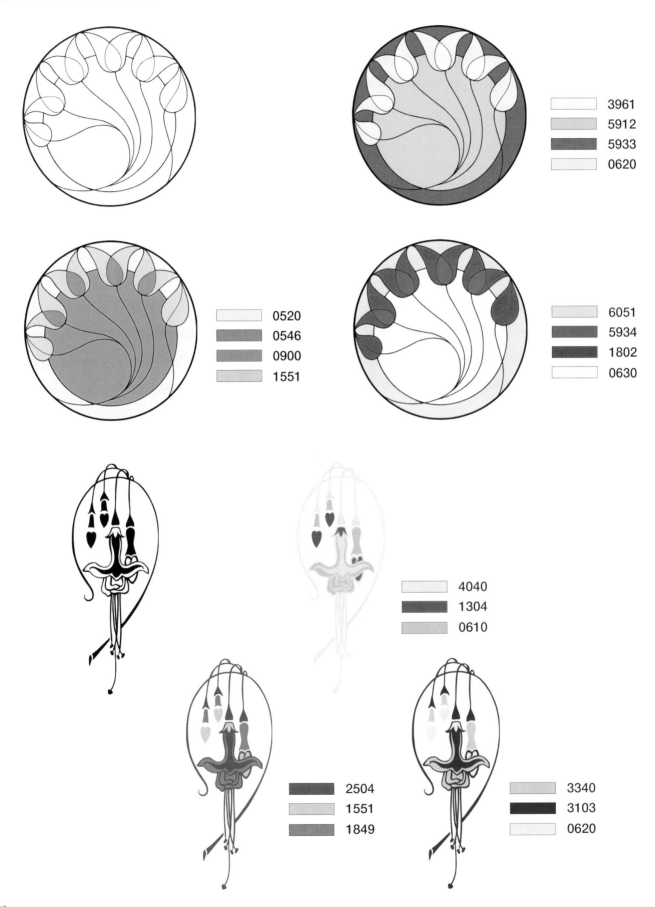

	3961
	5912
	5933
	0620

	0520
	0546
	0900
	1551

	6051
	5934
	1802
	0630

	4040
	1304
	0610

	2504
	1551
	1849

	3340
	3103
	0620

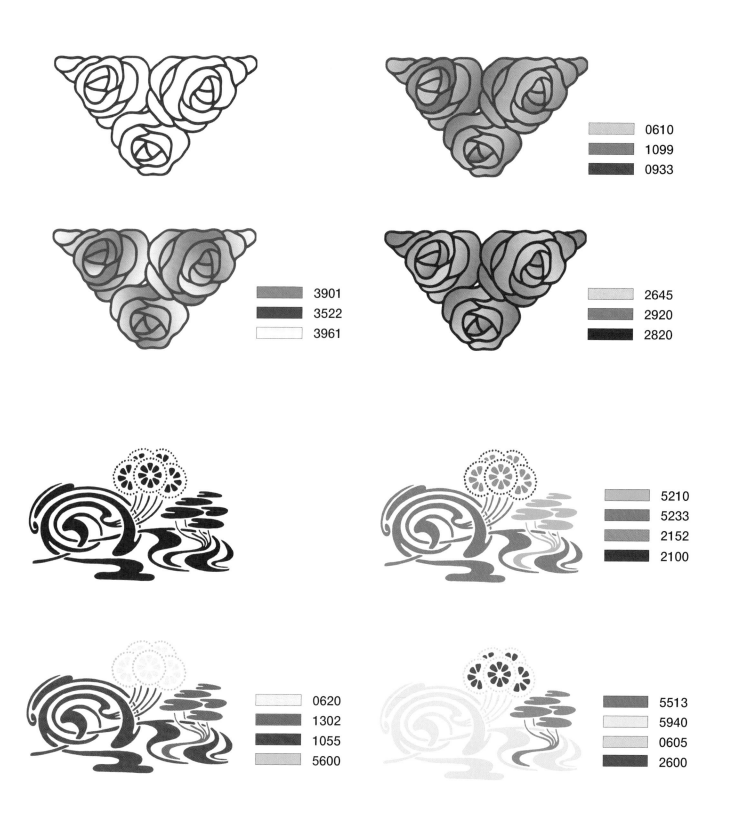

0610
1099
0933

3901
3522
3961

2645
2920
2820

5210
5233
2152
2100

0620
1302
1055
5600

5513
5940
0605
2600

	2640
	0506
	0842
	2712

	0620
	1302
	1055
	5600

	5210
	5233
	2152
	2100

	5832
	2640
	3631
	3040

	0532
	0345
	2022
	1421

	5542
	5940
	4250
	1120

■	3323
☐	0505
▦	0311
▦	5611

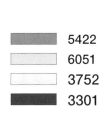

▦	5422
☐	6051
☐	3752
■	3301

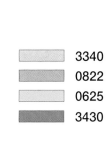

☐	3340
▦	0822
▦	0625
▦	3430

☐	2645
▦	3251
▦	1120

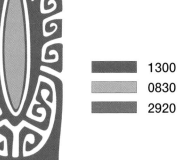

■	1902
☐	1860
▦	1850

▦	1300
▦	0830
▦	2920

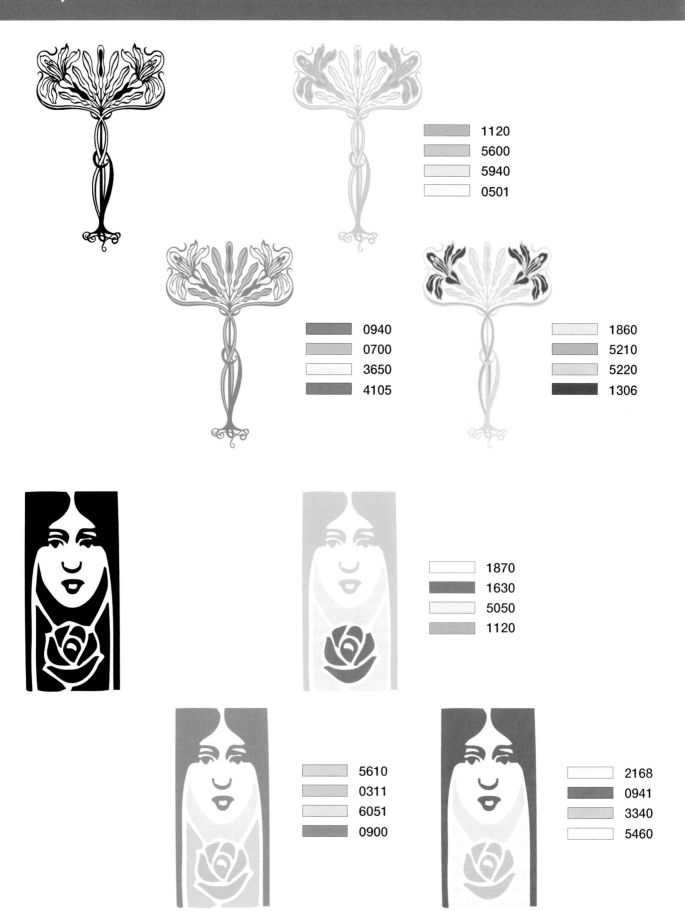

1120
5600
5940
0501

0940
0700
3650
4105

1860
5210
5220
1306

1870
1630
5050
1120

5610
0311
6051
0900

2168
0941
3340
5460

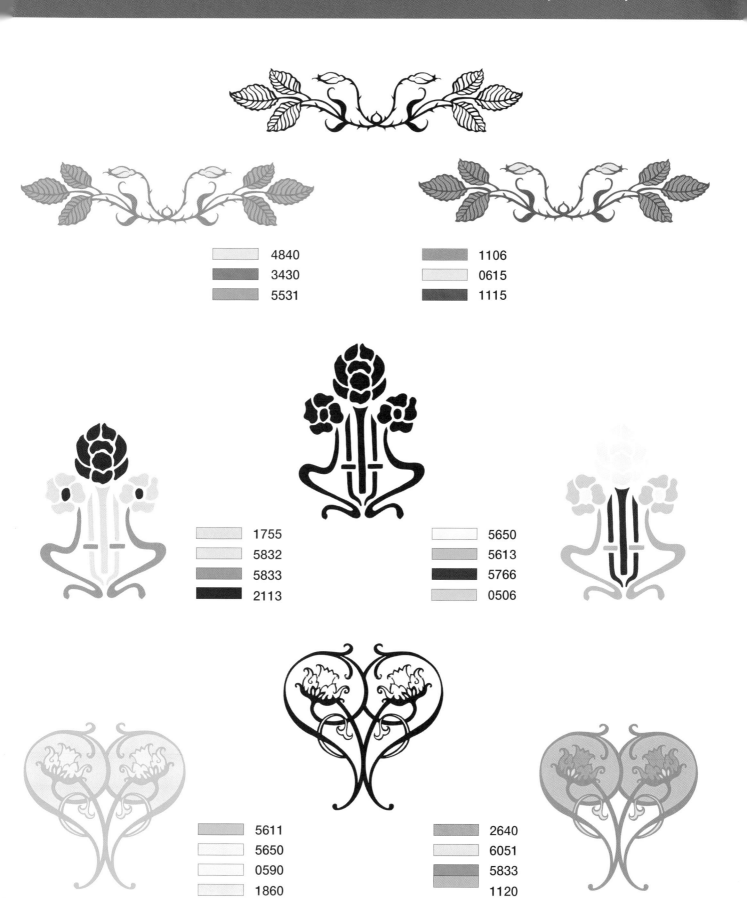

4840
3430
5531

1106
0615
1115

1755
5832
5833
2113

5650
5613
5766
0506

5611
5650
0590
1860

2640
6051
5833
1120

	5822
	1421

	0532
	3901

	0940
	2506

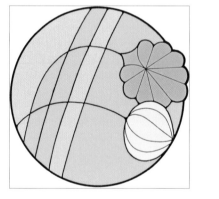

	1120
	5600
	5822
	0501

	0940
	0700
	3650
	4105

	1860
	5210
	5220
	1306